RAMADAN AND THE QURAN
Quran Stories for Little Hearts

by

S A N I Y A S N A I N   K H A N

Goodwordkidz

Helping you build a family of faith

The Prophet Muhammad ﷺ would often sit alone in the cave of Hira, near Makkah, to pray and think deeply, asking the Creator of the Heavens and earth for answers to the questions that surged through his mind.

What is man's true role in life? What does the Lord require of us? From where does man come, and where will he go after death? All alone the Prophet would remain deep in thought, surrounded by nature, seeking answers to all these profound questions.

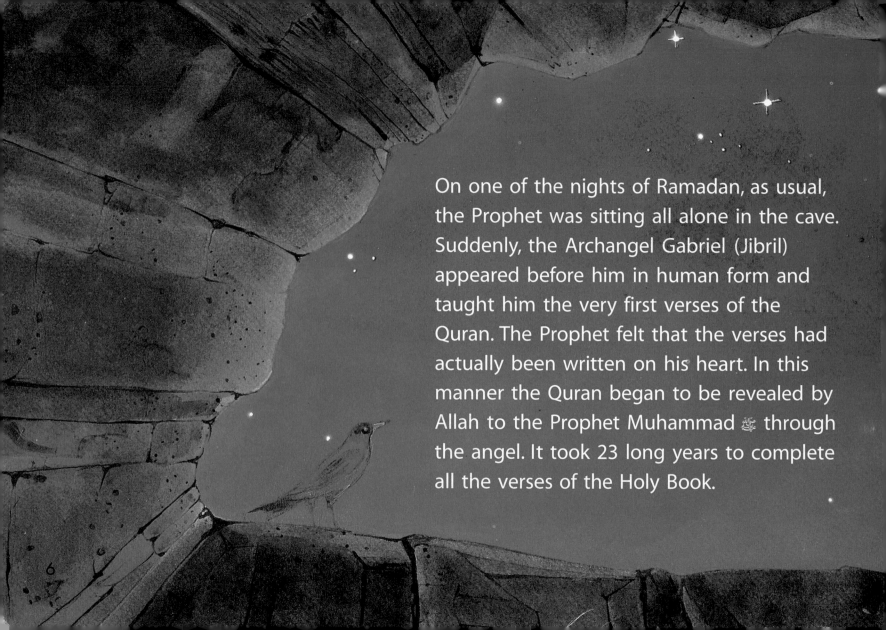

On one of the nights of Ramadan, as usual, the Prophet was sitting all alone in the cave. Suddenly, the Archangel Gabriel (Jibril) appeared before him in human form and taught him the very first verses of the Quran. The Prophet felt that the verses had actually been written on his heart. In this manner the Quran began to be revealed by Allah to the Prophet Muhammad ﷺ through the angel. It took 23 long years to complete all the verses of the Holy Book.

8

Being the true word of Allah in human language, the Quran is a book of learning for all mankind which will last forever.

9

It provides correct and understandable answers to all the central questions which arise in a mind which seeks answers. It serves as a guiding light, inspiring and leading the devout on the right path. The guidance given in the Quran is one of a kind and a great blessing to mankind from Allah, because it shows man the path to final success. It tells man how to behave, so that in the life after death he may enter Paradise, which is the final goal. Fasting is the path to it.

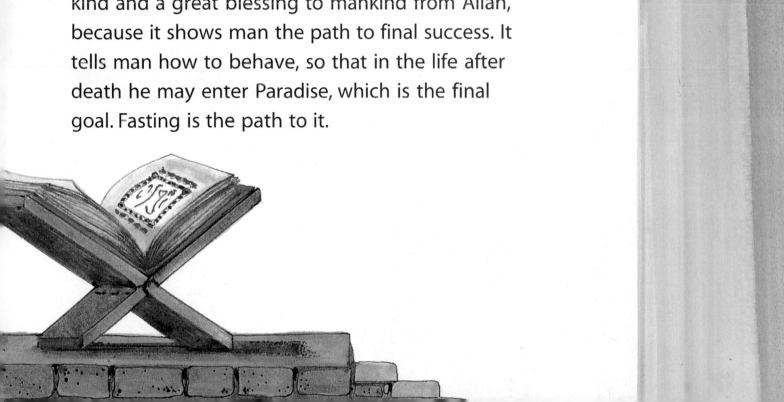

The month of Ramadan, therefore, is a yearly
reminder of this blessing which has no equal.

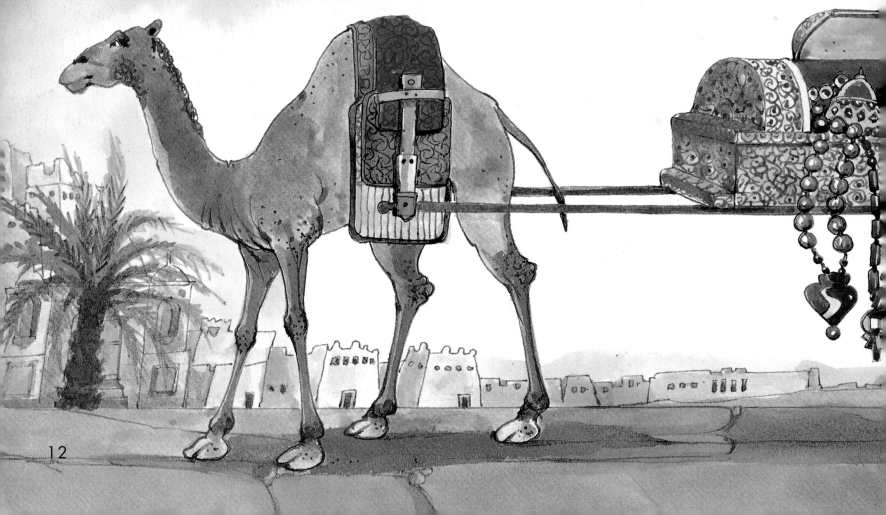

The celebration of the revelation of the Quran is not observed in the usual way, but is marked by not eating and drinking, and by showing gratitude to the Almighty, by various forms of charity. Fasting in this month is like saying 'Thank You' for the divine blessing.

This month is the very best one for reading and understanding the Quran. Special recitations of the Quran are held; it is also recited during the *tarawih* prayer.

The *tarawih* is actually the *tahajjud* prayer, which instead of being offered before dawn is offered after the *isha* prayer during this month to make things easy for godly people.

15

The Quran introduces the Creator and explains the bond between the Creator and His creations. A large part of the Quran deals with stories of the prophets, such as Adam, Nuh (Noah), Ibrahim (Abraham), Yusuf (Joseph), Musa (Moses), Isa (Jesus) and many more. Upon all of whom be peace. These stories teach lessons about what is good or bad for believers of all time.

Another part of the Quran talks about the Hereafter—which mainly describes in detail the delights of Paradise and the agony of Hell. Historical events, faith and religion, religious commandments, divine promises, prayers and matters of civil law are also dealt with.

When the Quran is read during the month of its revelation, Ramadan, it creates an atmosphere which reminds us of the time when the divine light from heaven fell upon the earth. The Quran is a guiding force in man's life. He earns his livelihood according to its rules. He bathes in the ocean of its life to cleanse his soul.

The Quran is a reward to His servants from Allah. And fasting is like saying 'Thank You' for the reward. Through fasting man makes himself worthy of being thankful to Allah. He obeys the command of Allah and so gains a keen awareness of how Allah is greater than everyone and everything else.

Having gone through a month's fasting, the believer is then able to lead a life of piety as laid down in the Qur'an.

Find Out More

To know more about the message and meaning of Allah's words, look up the following parts of the Quran which tells the story of Ramadan.

Surah al-Baqarah 2:183-185
Surah al-Alaq 96:1-5